Yosemite
National  Park

Nate Frisch

Published by
CREATIVE PAPERBACKS

P.O. Box 227, Mankato, Minnesota 56002
Creative Paperbacks is an imprint of The Creative Company
www.thecreativecompany.us

Design and production by Danny Nanos of Gilbert & Nanos
Art direction by Rita Marshall
Printed in the United States of America

Photographs by nps.gov, Shutterstock (Antonio Abrignani, Volha Ahranovich, artincamera,
Aspen Photo, Chris Bence, dashingstock, Dorn1530, Greg Epperson, Everett Collection,
Don Fink, fivespots, Harmony Gerber, Tom Grundy, J Hindman, javarman, Gregory Johnston,
Rob Kemp, Anne Kitzman, Radoslaw Lecyk, Marc Pagani Photography, Mayskyphoto, Jason Mintzer,
Morgan Lane Photography, Neftali, Vitalii Nesterchuk, pashabo, Pi-Lens, Linda Roberts,
Gary Saxe, Scenic Shutterbug, Nickolay Stanev, Amos Struck, Tatagatta,
Dan Tautan, TFoxFoto, upthebanner, Rick Whitacre, gary yim, Z.H.CHEN)

Library of Congress Cataloging-in-Publication Data

Frisch, Nate.
Yosemite National Park / by Nate Frisch.
p. cm. — (Preserving America)
Includes bibliographical references and index.
Summary: An exploration of Yosemite National Park, including how its mountainous landscape was formed,
its history of preservation, and tourist attractions such as the granite monolith called El Capitan.

ISBN 978-1-60818-199-5 (hardcover)
ISBN 978-0-89812-882-6 (pbk)
1. Yosemite National Park (Calif.)—Juvenile literature. I. Title.
F868.Y6F75 2013
979.4'47—dc23   2012023233

FIRST EDITION

2 4 6 8 9 7 5 3 1

Cover & page 3: *Yosemite Falls reflected in the Merced River; a kingsnake*

Yosemite National Park

Nate Frisch

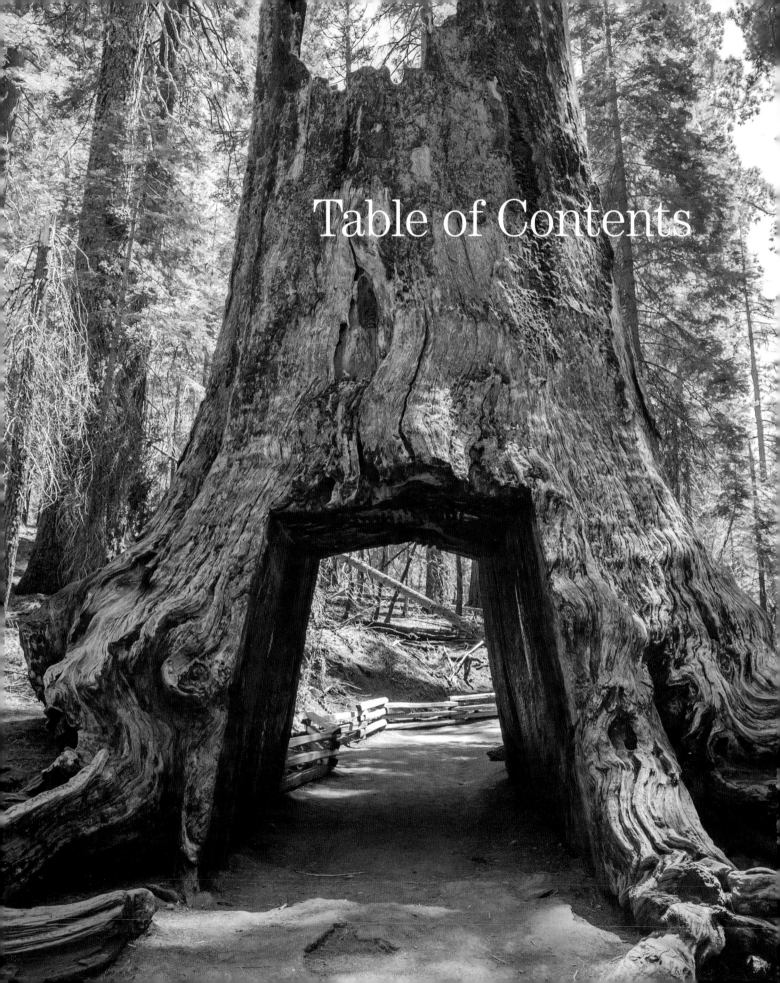

Table of Contents

TOWERING MOUNTAINS and glassy lakes. Churning rivers and dense forests. Lush prairies and baking deserts. The open spaces and natural wonders of the United States once seemed as limitless as they were diverse. But as human expansion and development increased in the 1800s, forests and prairies were replaced by settlements and agricultural lands. Waterways were diverted, wildlife was over-hunted, and the earth was scarred by mining. Fortunately, many Americans fought to preserve some of the country's vanishing wilderness. In 1872, Yellowstone National Park was established, becoming the first true national park in the world and paving the way for future preservation efforts. In 1901, Theodore Roosevelt became U.S. president. He once stated, "There can be no greater issue than that of conservation in this country," and during his presidency, Roosevelt signed five national parks into existence. The National Park Service (NPS) was created in 1916 to manage the growing number of U.S. parks, including Yosemite. Throughout the decades, this Western land's larger-than-life mountains, waterfalls, and trees have endeared it to visitors from around the globe and made Yosemite a classic among America's national parks.

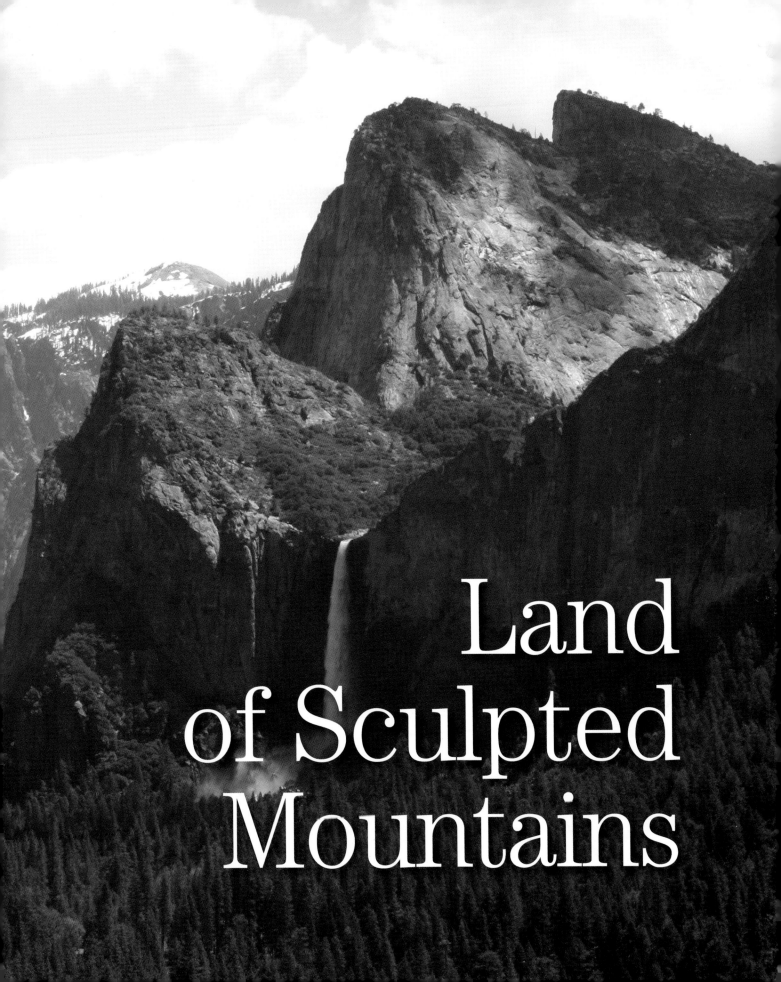

Land
of Sculpted
Mountains

Yosemite is characterized by sky-piercing mountain peaks and plunging waterfalls. The creation of these awe-inspiring features involved the collaboration of many dramatic and powerful forces of nature. The basic building material of the Yosemite region is granite, which is formed from molten rock that cools within the earth. As it slowly cools to a solid, large and interlocking crystals are formed, which means that granite lacks the layering effect found in many other types of rock. The same durability and consistency that makes granite a preferred stone for countertops and gravestones has allowed the Yosemite region to exhibit cliff faces that ascend straight up for thousands of feet.

Falling rocks are common along Yosemite's mountainsides; in 2012, the threat caused the park to close some cabins and campsites

Around the time that dinosaurs went extinct some 65 million years ago, less resilient rock on the earth's surface had **eroded** away, exposing granite throughout the Yosemite area. However, the land was generally low and flat, and it wasn't until about 25 million years ago that actual mountains began to form. This process was set in motion by a **fault** in Earth's crust. The incredibly massive chunk of crust on the western side of the break began tilting toward the west, thus raising its eastern edge. The result we see today is the Sierra Nevadas, a mountain range extending 400 miles (643 km) along California's eastern border. The range features steep eastern slopes and relatively gradual western slopes and is home to the region now called Yosemite.

While this tilting process was extremely slow—and continues to this day—even minor slants early on triggered another phase in the shaping of Yosemite. Water that had once been scattered across the region in lakes and ponds began trickling to the west. As time passed and the slopes increased, streams began to flow with ever-increasing force. Over millions of years, this water flow carved canyons and gorges into the defiant granite.

Two or three million years ago, a drop in global temperatures and the still-increasing elevation of the Sierra Nevadas led to the formation of glaciers in the area. Tons upon tons of snow compressed under its own weight, creating massive sheets of ice in the mountains. The glaciers typically formed at high altitudes, and tremendous gravitational force then slowly pulled the icy behemoths down the mountain slopes. As the glaciers descended, loose or dislodged stone was dragged along, further enhancing the glaciers' earth-carving power.

Over thousands of years, glaciers defined the landscape, often expanding the erosion already caused by the rivers and streams. Yet, unlike water or wind that wear away only the most superficial layers of earth and create rounded edges and gradual slants, the unstoppable masses of ice and stone gouged through solid rock, leaving sheer cliffs of bare granite in their wake. Yosemite Valley and its many waterfalls and smooth stone faces were created in this way.

No other national park in America can match Yosemite's impressive waterways and waterfalls (Tuolumne Falls pictured)

Among the valley's most prominent peaks are El Capitan, Half Dome, and Glacier Point. El Capitan is an enormous **monolith** of bare granite featuring a blunt peak, curved, sloping edges to the north and east, and steep, sharply defined faces to the south and west. Half Dome is appropriately named, as the northwestern side of the rounded peak has been shorn off, leaving a vast, flat wall that can reflect sunsets in spectacular fashion. Glacier Point is remarkable not so much for its own appearance but rather for the vantage point the clifftop provides from 3,000 feet (914 m) above the Yosemite Valley floor.

Yosemite Valley also contains a high concentration of towering waterfalls such as Yosemite Falls, where water from Yosemite Creek plummets 2,425 feet (739 m) over the course of 3 drops, making the falls the tallest in North America. Ribbon Fall, which flows over the western side of El Capitan, has a single vertical drop of 1,612 feet (491 m).

While the top of El Capitan can be reached by a rear hiking route, rock climbers take the hard way up, along the cliff's face

Bridalveil Fall drops a comparatively short 620 feet (189 m), but it is highly visible from the western mouth of Yosemite Valley, and wind blowing into the valley often scatters the falling water into a showering mist. Each of these falls and several others feed into the valley's Merced River.

Besides their part in carving the terrain, glaciers played another role in defining the landscape of Yosemite. As Earth's climate warmed again some 10,000 years ago, the ice sheets melted, leaving behind piles of the rubble they had collected. More notably, the many basins the glaciers had created throughout the region were filled by the glaciers' melting ice, creating most of Yosemite's more than 250 lakes. This, in turn, helped to support the region's diverse **ecosystem**.

Yosemite's elevation ranges from about 2,000 to more than 13,000 feet (610–3,962 m) above sea level, and the varying altitudes accommodate 5 distinct zones of vegetation. From the lowest elevations to the highest, these are the foothill-woodland zone, lower montane forest, upper montane forest, subalpine forest, and the alpine zone.

The foothill-woodland zone is characterized by hot summers, mild winters, and little precipitation all year. Vegetation in this zone mostly takes the form of shrubs and small trees. The lower montane forest has a slightly cooler temperature and more precipitation, with several feet of snow accumulating in the winter. These two lowest zones are home to most of the Yosemite region's largest animals, including black bears, mule deer, and coyotes.

The upper montane and subalpine forests have relatively short summers and cold, snowy winters. Including the lower montane forest, these three forest zones dominate most of the Yosemite region and primarily feature pines, firs, and cedars interspersed with **deciduous** trees, including various oak species. The lower, western forests support

Bridalveil Fall gushes water in the spring, but during drier seasons, the thin layer of falling water often takes the form of mist

the widest variety of trees, including pockets of giant sequoias—the largest living tree species in the world. Although not as tall as some other redwood types, sequoias are thicker in the trunk. The world's largest known specimen is about 275 feet (84 m) tall with a trunk more than 30 feet (9 m) in diameter at the base. Sequoias are also among the longest-lived trees on the planet, and a Yosemite tree known as the "Grizzly Giant" is believed to be around 2,000 years old. Farther up the valley walls and mountain slopes are thinner forests mostly composed of pine species such as the gnarled foxtail pine, which can withstand cold temperatures and has the uncanny ability to establish a root system in seemingly barren rock.

Yosemite's alpine zone makes up the region's highest elevations. Beginning around 9,500 feet (2,896 m), it is generally devoid of trees, and only patches of quick-growing grasses and small plants sprout on the mountaintops during the short summer. Among the relatively few animals that live above the tree line are the rare Sierra Nevada bighorn sheep and the peregrine falcon, the fastest-flying bird in the world.

Aside from their countless trees, Yosemite's woodland and forest zones contain many meadows, which are found on mountain **plateaus** as well as on valley floors. These grassy expanses provide vital food resources to wildlife in the region, and most of Yosemite's more than 400 **vertebrate** species are found in areas where meadows, forests, and lakes or streams are all close together. This includes many of the park's 90 mammal species such as mountain lions, red foxes, black bears, and mule deer. Yosemite's bird population includes several owls and many songbirds. Noteworthy reptiles include the venomous western rattlesnake, the multicolored California mountain kingsnake, and the western fence lizard. Amphibians such as the Sierra Nevada yellow-legged frog and the Yosemite toad are **endemic** to the Sierra Nevadas. Yosemite's relatively small list of native fish species includes the rainbow trout and Sacramento sucker.

Mule deer in mountainous areas such as the Sierra Nevadas move to lower elevations in the winter to find warmer temperatures

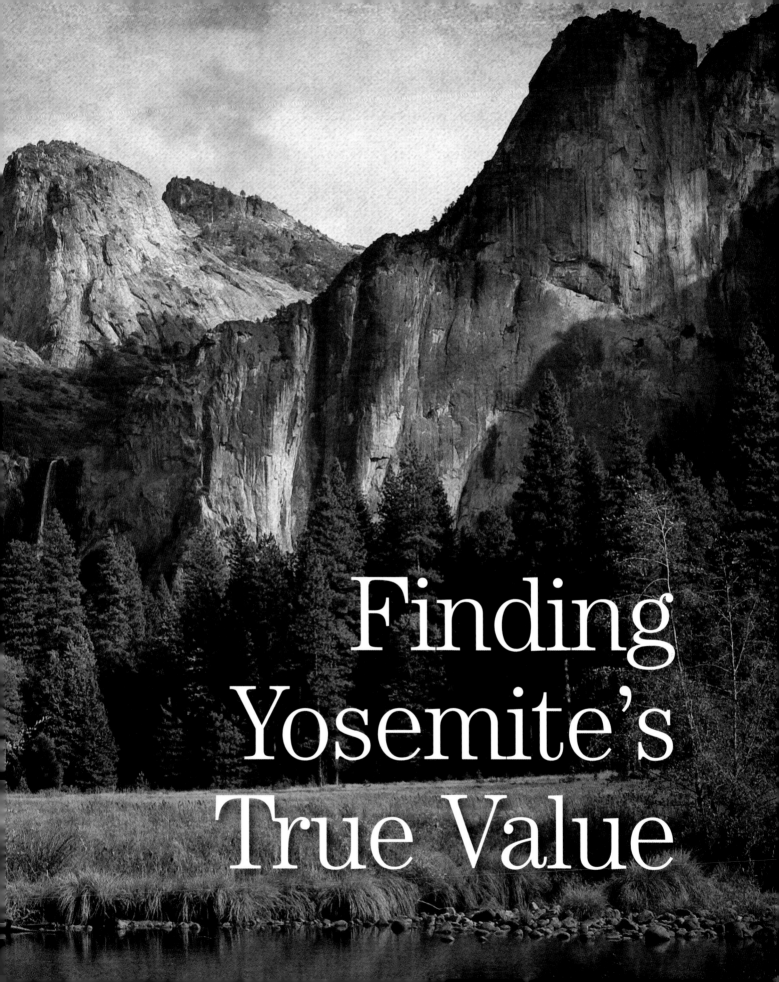

Finding Yosemite's True Value

American Indian legends passed down over many generations assert that the native people who inhabited the Yosemite region were created there and had resided there since the beginning of the land's existence. The first actual evidence of human life in the area dates back about 5,000 years, but little is known of those first hunter-gatherers.

Around 3,000 years ago, a sudden shift in native culture—from a **nomadic** lifestyle to one of more permanent settlement—seems to have occurred, indicating a change of inhabitants. The first known and named residents of Yosemite were members of the Miwok or Paiute tribes, who called themselves Ahwahneechees, which meant "dwellers of the gaping mouth," a reference to Yosemite Valley.

Among the first white explorers likely to have ventured into Yosemite were a group of frontiersmen led by Joseph Reddeford Walker. Their 1833 voyage into the Sierra Nevadas was not well-documented or recorded, and it is not certain they were even in Yosemite, but upon returning to developed settlements in California, they described a vast valley with nearby groves of giant trees. White visitors to the area remained scarce until 1848, when gold was discovered at a sawmill called Sutter's Mill about 150 miles (241 km) northwest of Yosemite. This ignited the famous California Gold Rush and drew swarms of gold-seekers to the area, including Yosemite.

This 1934 postage stamp celebrating Yosemite was released 70 years after the land first received government protection

Conflict soon erupted between encroaching prospectors and the area's native tribes, and the U.S. government began attempting to move the tribes onto reservations. Some of the tribes resisted, and violence escalated. Following attacks on trading posts by Indians in 1851, a **militia** of about 200 men was formed in Mariposa, California. Led by James D. Savage, this "Mariposa Battalion" was created to force the surrender of all

Indians in the area. Several tribes complied and signed treaties. The Ahwahneechees were among the tribes that did not, so about 130 soldiers entered Yosemite Valley. They eventually captured the Ahwahneechee chief Tenaya near the lake that now bears his name and forced the tribe off the land and onto a reservation. The relocation of the Ahwahneechees signaled the end of a cultural era in Yosemite.

As white settlers took over Yosemite, use of the region and its resources changed drastically. Gold mining was attempted in Yosemite but was generally unsuccessful, and as gold fever diminished, logging and ranching emerged as the region's primary enterprises. Livestock grazed in the lower valleys, while massive trees were felled higher up. The giant sequoias were tempting targets for loggers but provided poor lumber, often shattering into splinters when they fell. Many were cut

Some of the first travelers to Yosemite Valley cared less about the natural wonders than about the prospect of gold

A small number of people made themselves at home in Yosemite in the decades before the region was given park status

down anyway, but their brittle nature may have ultimately prevented the enormous trees from being wiped out.

While Yosemite was initially valued for its profitable resources, a different perception of the region soon began to emerge, thanks in large part to James Hutchings. An English immigrant and **entrepreneur**, Hutchings had traveled to California to find gold. In 1855, he toured Yosemite Valley and became one of its first settlers. The following year, he published the first edition of his *Hutchings' California Magazine*, featuring descriptions and illustrations of Yosemite Valley's many spectacles. Hutchings published 60 editions of his magazine from 1856 to 1861, with each copy providing more details of the region and accounts of his own adventures within it.

A man named Galen Clark followed a similar path. Clark was fascinated by the giant sequoias in Yosemite's Mariposa Grove, and in 1857, he built a cabin positioned between the grove and Yosemite Valley. He wrote newspaper articles describing the enormous trees and lobbying for their protection. Both Clark and Hutchings not only promoted the region through words and print, but they also played host to many early visitors, with Hutchings going so far as to operate a hotel.

As public interest in Yosemite increased, growing numbers of artists, photographers, scientists, journalists, and general outdoor enthusiasts visited the valley. They marveled at the region's majestic waterfalls, lofty peaks, and varied life forms, and their own paintings, photographs, discoveries, and written accounts of Yosemite fanned the flames of its popularity in the late 1850s and early 1860s. The concept of conservation was somewhat revolutionary at the time, but an overwhelming sentiment was born—that Yosemite Valley should be preserved in its natural state rather than exploited for its resources.

In 1864, California senator John Conness introduced a bill in the U.S. Congress to preserve and protect Yosemite Valley and the Mariposa Grove. The bill was signed by president Abraham Lincoln, and the two regions were put under the control of the state of California to be managed as a protected public area. This effectively (though unofficially) created America's first state park.

Hutchings and Clark remained important figures during the park's early years. In a way, Hutchings's own publicity of Yosemite came back to haunt him. With Yosemite Valley now considered the property of the state, Hutchings had a home and hotel in the park that he could no longer keep. He had wanted Yosemite to succeed in becoming a protected area but not at his own expense. After 10 years of legal disputes, Hutchings received a large settlement from the state of California and left the valley in 1875. Years later, however, he would write a book about Yosemite and even work as a park official for a short time. Clark worked

As in many national parks, much of the wildlife in Yosemite is acclimated to humans, making up-close photography possible

for the park during most of its first 33 years of existence. He also continued to advocate for further protection of the larger Yosemite region, of which Yosemite Valley and the Mariposa Grove were only a small part.

Aiding Clark's ongoing efforts in the later 1800s was an increasingly prominent figure named John Muir. The Scottish-born Muir was an amateur naturalist and conservationist whose natural curiosity carried him farther than his limited formal education could. He was an eccentric man who never shaved and thus had a large beard, and during his time in Yosemite, he was known to put himself in harm's way during storms and encounters with wildlife in order to better understand nature.

Muir first came to Yosemite in 1868, and he recorded his impressions in writing, noting, "No temple made with hands can compare with

In 2007, a life-size statue was erected at the Yosemite Visitor Center as a means of honoring famed naturalist John Muir

Yosemite. Every rock in its walls seems to glow with life." Muir found work first as a shepherd, then as a laborer at a sawmill. Ironically, he came to view both livestock grazing and logging as major threats to the larger Yosemite ecosystem and later spoke out against them. Muir became increasingly knowledgeable about the region and began writing articles about glaciers and how they had shaped the landscape of Yosemite. He also wrote about forests and wildlife in the park and beyond and about how they were being destroyed or depleted, in part because of a lack of government protection.

Muir's criticisms did not sit well with the ranchers and loggers of the region and put him at odds with some politicians. However, his knowledge, poetic writing style, and pure intentions endeared him to the general public and impressed a number of prominent figures in various professional fields, including Robert Underwood, editor of the influential *Century Magazine*. In 1889, Underwood began publishing Muir's proposals for a Yosemite national park. Public support for the further preservation skyrocketed, and on October 1, 1890, Yosemite National Park was established, adding more than 1,000 square miles (2,590 sq km) of land around Yosemite Valley and the Mariposa Grove.

The federal government put the U.S. Army in charge of the park, and the military presence was effective in preventing illegal grazing, lumber harvesting, and poaching. The army constructed roads, trails, and park structures and was charged with managing wildfires. Troops also served as park hosts and sources of information for guests. This multifaceted role was the precursor to that of today's park rangers (even the style of hats worn by rangers has remained the same), and Yosemite—one of only four national parks at the time—helped establish a model for America's future parks.

Mariposa Grove contains a few hundred mature sequoia trees, including a 285-foot (87 m) giant that is the tallest in Yosemite

Bears,
Dams, and Fire

Although Yosemite National Park was officially born in 1890, it was not actually the same park it is today, because Yosemite Valley and the Mariposa Grove—which had been established as a state park in 1864—remained under the control of California. Only the land surrounding the valley and the grove made up the national park and were the federal government's responsibility. The army had the national park well under control, but it had no power in the state park, where facilities seemed neglected, and higher concentrations of tourists bound by fewer regulations were leaving natural habitats polluted, trampled, and otherwise disturbed.

John Muir, who founded the Sierra Club environmental organization in 1892, continued to push for higher standards in Yosemite and lobbied to have the entire region placed under federal control. In 1903, president Theodore Roosevelt visited Yosemite and toured the park with Muir, seeing firsthand the contrast between the state-operated and army-controlled portions of Yosemite. In 1906, Roosevelt signed a bill that put Yosemite Valley and the Mariposa Grove under federal management and created the single unified park that exists today.

Around the same time that these governmental matters were being sorted out, an ecological problem was introduced into Yosemite. Starting in the late 1800s and continuing until 1990, an estimated 30 million nonnative game fish were stocked in the park's lakes and streams. Although it took a long time for park officials to realize it, this process led to the drastic reduction of native species. One such example is the Sierra Nevada yellow-legged frog, which was once abundant in many of Yosemite's lakes and ponds—aquatic habitats that, owing to their isolation, never contained fish. Populations of the frogs have been reduced about 95 percent, since the amphibians have become prey to the

For many thousands of years, Sierra Nevada yellow-legged frogs lived in relative safety in lakes that had no fish

introduced fish. The stocking of fish was finally stopped in 1991, but most of the nonnative species introduced previously still exist in Yosemite.

Another more trivial but notable Yosemite issue also emerged in the late 1800s. It began when a man named James McCauley pushed a camp-fire off the cliff of Glacier Point. The red-hot logs and coals plummeted more than half a mile (800 m) to the cliff's base, much to the delight of onlookers below. McCauley soon began charging admission for the night-time spectacle, and when enough customers gathered, McCauley's sons would send burning embers cascading down, emitting showers of sparks as they banked off subtle rock outcroppings. The event was continued in the early 1900s by the owners of Yosemite's Glacial Point Hotel as a means of attracting business. In 1968, the "Fire Fall" was finally banned by the NPS, which determined that the stunt was at odds with Yosemite's purpose of encouraging appreciation of natural wonders.

A more serious matter arose in 1906, when the building of a dam on Yosemite's Tuolumne River was proposed. The purpose of the dam was to supply water and **hydroelectric power** to the city of San Francisco.

It took eight years to build the O'Shaughnessy Dam, which created an artificial lake used to provide drinking water to San Francisco

The Hetch Hetchy Reservoir has long stirred up heated debates about how to balance urban needs with natural preservation

Environmentalists—including Muir and members of the Sierra Club—who opposed the dam's construction claimed it would compromise the natural landscape and ecosystem of the region. The portion of the park that would become flooded was the Hetch Hetchy Valley, which Muir and others considered to be among Yosemite's greatest features.

In the end, the conservationists lost the battle when Congress authorized the dam's construction in 1913. When the O'Shaughnessy Dam was completed in 1923, the Hetch Hetchy Valley became the Hetch Hetchy **Reservoir**. The reservoir is impressive in its own right, but the dam is still controversial. Environmentalists have continued to lobby for its removal, but the California Department of Water Resources claims that taking the dam down now and establishing new water and power supplies would cost billions of dollars.

For several years in the 1930s, Yosemite management carried out a popular but ill-advised practice of feeding the park's bears. Park workers dumped food waste in specified feeding sites in the belief that it would keep the bears away from campgrounds and other places where people congregated. These "bear pits" became popular and promoted tourist attractions. Eventually, park officials realized that this unnatural feeding practice made bears lose their inborn fear of humans. Bears that become so emboldened are potentially dangerous, and many such bears had to be killed every year.

Yosemite's modern bear management policies stand in sharp contrast to those of yesteryear. Dumpsters in the park are heavy-duty and have lids with latches. Every campsite has a metal "bear-proof" box for food storage. Campers are required to use these, as bears have been known to break car windows or pry into vehicles and trailers. Rangers occasionally use such extreme tactics as shooting bears with rubber

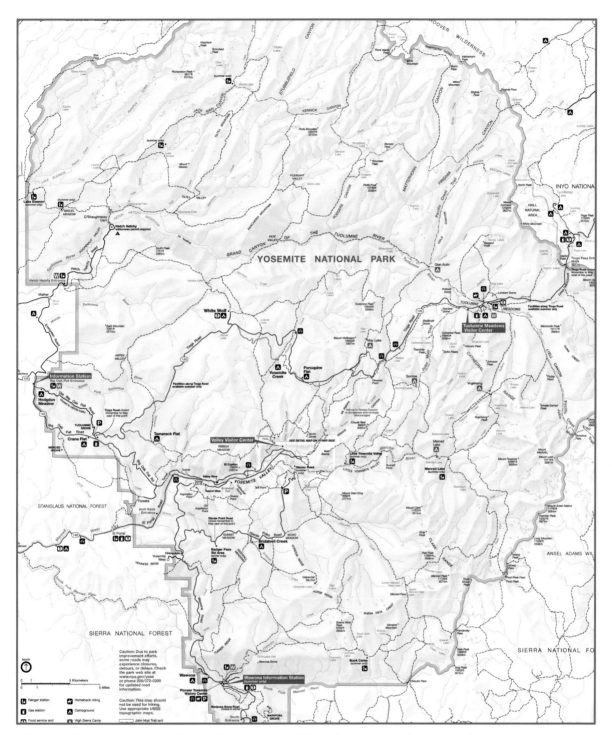

slugs or beanbags fired from shotguns to drive them away from roads or other areas where they are in danger or pose a threat to visitors. Some of Yosemite's bears are tagged or wear radio collars to allow park workers to monitor them more closely. Park management has even gone so far as

Although the park covers about 1,200 square miles (3,110 sq km), most visitors hone in on Yosemite Valley

Planes are called into action against big wildfires, with the aircraft dropping fire-retardant chemicals where they are needed most

to collect **DNA** samples from some of the tagged bears. By doing so, they can identify bears that may be responsible for damage in campgrounds or other problems by collecting hair or saliva from the "crime scene."

Another reversal in Yosemite park policy involved forest fire management. In the 1930s, the NPS and U.S. Forest Service developed a policy of strict wildfire suppression and took prompt action to squelch any forest fires. In the 1970s, this stance on fire prevention became less stringent. One reason for the shift was that sending firefighters out at the first sign of smoke was costly. More significantly, people began to recognize that fire was a natural and necessary factor in maintaining balanced ecosystems with diverse plant growth.

During the fire-suppression era, Yosemite's forests changed. Forest floors became crowded with small trees, which prevented the growth of grasses and shrubs. The forests also began to take over the region's meadows, further depleting wildlife habitat and food sources. Some trees, including giant sequoias, release their seeds only under extreme heat, and those seeds need open, fertile soil to sprout. These trees were not reproducing in the absence of fires.

Yet another consequence of strict fire suppression is that dead plant debris accumulates over time and—along with the more numerous small trees—creates large-scale tinder capable of fueling fires far more destructive than would naturally occur. In 1990, fires ignited by lightning consumed more than 30 square miles (88 sq km) of Yosemite forests, causing a temporary closure of the park. Many people speculated that the severity would have been reduced had more **prescribed burns** been conducted in Yosemite. Today, the park's policy includes prescribed burns as well as containing but not immediately dousing naturally occurring forest fires. This has led to a park that looks more like it did a century ago and the resurgence of animals—such as the California spotted owl and northern flying squirrel—that survive better in forests less cluttered with small trees.

In an effort to reduce air pollution, noise, and traffic congestion on Yosemite's roads, the park introduced a fleet of 18 hybrid electric-diesel shuttle buses in 2005. These new buses produce less than half the fuel emissions of the diesel buses they replaced. By running more quietly and reducing car traffic, the buses lessen human impact on wildlife near the roadways and improve the visitor experience as well. The idea has been proposed that, during the summer, some roads be limited to buses alone or that visitors who are not camping or lodging in the park be required to use bus services instead of driving within the park. While such mandatory bus use may or may not happen in the years to come, the quality of the new buses and the low-stress service they provide have many visitors gladly leaving their own vehicles behind.

In its history as a park, Yosemite has been hit by numerous wildfires—some started by lightning, others by human carelessness

The
Rewards of
Conservation

Yosemite hosts more than 3.5 million visitors each year, making it among America's most popular national parks. A big reason for this popularity—aside from the park's awe-inspiring sights—is its nearness to the huge metropolitan areas of San Francisco and Los Angeles. This geographic advantage allows many big-city visitors to come for just a weekend or even a single day.

Also contributing to the high visitor numbers is Yosemite's warm climate and the long tourist season it permits. Daily high temperatures at lower elevations average close to 90 °F (32 °C) in the summer and 50 °F (10 °C) in the winter. Higher altitudes are often significantly cooler, but that does not affect the majority of tourists, who tend to limit their visits exclusively to Yosemite Valley, a segment which accounts for less than 1 percent of the park's total area.

June, July, and August make up Yosemite's busiest season, and campgrounds and lodges are often filled to capacity during summer weekends. Late spring and early fall are also popular times to visit. The drier conditions of fall make for pleasant camping and firm hiking trails, while the wetter spring season has the distinct advantage of more impressive waterfalls. Winter visitors are limited to some extent by snow-induced road closures throughout much of the park. However, Yosemite Valley remains accessible by vehicle, and tourists can still traverse closed roads on cross-country skis or snowshoes. Frozen lakes and rivers also provide ice-skating opportunities, and the park offers downhill skiing and sledding at Badger Pass.

Regardless of the season, sightseeing is the primary activity in the park, which explains the extreme popularity of Yosemite Valley. Merely by driving

Although much of California is known for its sunny warmth, Yosemite's higher elevations have abundant snows for winter recreation

or by riding buses through the valley, visitors are able to see a multitude of sights worthy of postcards, including the park's most prominent waterfalls and cliff formations as well as streams, meadows, forests, and wildlife. The seven-square-mile (18 sq km) valley also contains several visitor centers that feature information desks and exhibits about the park's geology, plant and animal life, and American Indian history. Some locations offer interpretive programs, and guests can also buy books and souvenirs at gift shops. Larger general stores exist throughout the park, and some sell groceries and rent recreational equipment such as bicycles.

Another Yosemite location accessible by vehicle is Glacier Point. With an elevation of 7,214 feet (2,199 m), this clifftop overlooks Yosemite Valley and provides arguably the best view in the park, including a striking profile of the Half Dome formation backdropped by the

Tenaya Lake can provide a great ice-skating surface in the winter, if the frozen waters are not covered by deep snow

park's tallest peak, Mount Lyell, far in the distance. This vantage point is so renowned that the California state quarter depicts John Muir standing on Glacier Point gazing toward Half Dome. Glacier Point also offers panoramic views of several waterfalls, including the nearly half-mile-high (800 m) Yosemite Falls.

Roads also lead to the Mariposa Grove and its giant sequoia trees in the southern reaches of the park and to the Hetch Hetchy Reservoir to the northwest. The Tioga Road winds from east to west roughly through the center of Yosemite. This roadway covers higher elevations, and while it lacks the spectacular individual features found in Yosemite Valley, it provides wide-open views of high-range meadows and forests, snowy peaks, and mountain lakes such as Lake Tenaya.

For tourists interested in leaving roads behind, there are about 800 miles (1,287 km) of hiking trails spread throughout Yosemite National Park. Yosemite Valley contains several easy hikes that are less than a mile (1.6 km) one way and lead to such popular sites as Mirror Lake and the bases of Yosemite and Bridalveil falls. At the other extreme, strenuous trails more than 10 miles (16 km) long are also common. Yosemite's intermediate hikes include the popular Mist Trail. Many guests combine hiking with bird-watching or photography.

Yosemite is world-famous for its rock climbing opportunities and is largely responsible for the development of the sport in the U.S. The park draws thousands of climbers who spend hours or even days at a time scaling Yosemite's sheer cliffs. Those who spend more than a day on a rock face will spend nights sleeping in a bivouac—a sort of suspended cot. El Capitan and Half Dome in particular are favorite climbing locations, and tourists in the valley below often use binoculars to zoom in on climbers who otherwise look like insignificant specks on the giant cliff walls.

Yosemite rock climbing is a thrill that requires considerable skill, teamwork, and dependable equipment (Yosemite Falls pictured)

The beautiful Merced River is a hotspot for rafting, swimming, and other forms of aquatic recreation in Yosemite

Yosemite's lakes and rivers offer recreational opportunities in the forms of swimming, boating, and fishing. Swimming is permitted anywhere in the park except the Hetch Hetchy Reservoir or above waterfalls. When water levels and temperatures are appropriate, rafts may be rented and used on portions of the Merced River in Yosemite Valley. Guests can also use their own rafts, kayaks, and canoes on the river, and Lake Tenaya is likewise popular among kayakers and canoeists. Yosemite's lakes and rivers contain several species of trout and bass, and fishing licenses and angling supplies can be purchased at various shops throughout the park.

During warmer months, guided horse and mule rides are offered in many areas of the park, including Yosemite Valley and the Mariposa Grove. Ride options are available for both novice and experienced riders and range from two-hour trips to multi-day packages in which guests spend nights camping along the trail. Reservations are necessary, especially for the longer treks. Guests may bring their own horses or mules to ride on approved trails. The animals can be kept in one of Yosemite's three horse camps, or advance arrangements may be made for overnight boarding in the park's stables.

Guests spending 1 or more nights in Yosemite have 14 campgrounds and 1,400 campsites from which to choose. Most campgrounds have running water and accommodate RVs (tents are allowed in all sites), but none of the campgrounds provides electricity, RV hookups, or showers. Shower facilities are available only at the Curry Village & Housekeeping Camp in Yosemite Valley. About half of the park's campgrounds take reservations, while the others operate on a first-come, first-served basis. Reservations are recommended for visitors planning to come on summer weekends, especially if they want to be in Yosemite Valley. **Backcountry** camping is another popular option, and visitors eager to venture off the beaten pathways are not confined to designated backcountry campsites.

Visitors without their own overnight shelter have eight lodging locations from which to choose in Yosemite, ranging from the plush Ahwahnee Hotel to the rustic Curry Village & Housekeeping Camp. The appearance of the Ahwahnee is striking—a castle-like structure of stone and wood that features large windows. Its earthy exterior makes it look very much at home in Yosemite Valley, but high-class services and fancy interior furnishings make the Ahwahnee the most luxurious hotel in

Visitors looking to escape Yosemite crowds or take a break from more rigorous activities might try their luck in catching trout

the park. Past guests have included U.S. presidents, English royalty, and Hollywood celebrities.

Also located in Yosemite Valley, Curry Village & Housekeeping Camp began operating in 1899 and remains among the park's most popular establishments today. Appealing to a very different customer base from The Ahwahnee, Curry Village & Housekeeping Camp offers basic accommodations, including canvas tent cabins and primitive wood cabins. Yosemite also features several restaurants that, like the lodging options, vary greatly in price and elegance.

While Yosemite offers certain modern amenities that some people may find out of place in a national park, about 95 percent of Yosemite National Park's land is congressionally designated as wilderness, meaning that about 1,100 square miles (2,849 sq km) of natural environment cannot be altered to contain any roads or other man-made developments. After all, the natural wonders of Yosemite were what captured the imaginations of its earliest visitors, and they will continue to call people to the Sierra Nevadas long into the future.

Yosemite has some fantastically luxurious lodging, but many visitors still prefer to end a day of hiking with a night under the stars

Banded Mountain Stranglers

The California mountain kingsnake is one of Yosemite's 13 snake species and is certainly its most colorful, exhibiting bands of red, black, and white. Kingsnakes can grow to four feet (1.2 m) in length, but most are about half that. They kill prey by constriction, or suffocation through squeezing, and eat mostly small rodents, lizards, and young birds or eggs. They will also eat other snakes, including Yosemite's western rattlesnakes. California mountain kingsnakes are active during the day but generally remain under the rocks and shrubs that are part of their usual habitat. Although these reptiles prefer dry ground, they are versatile in their movement, able to climb trees and swim as well.

Remarkable River Walkers

To see an American dipper just standing along a riverbank is no particular thrill. This medium-sized songbird has drab gray coloring, and its high-pitched calls are pleasant but nondescript. What makes the American dipper remarkable is its habit of diving into swiftly moving, rocky streams and walking along the bottom as it seeks out aquatic insects, insect larvae, or tiny fish. Long, gripping toes enable the bird

to withstand the river current, its closeable nostrils are watertight, and see-through inner eyelids enable it to see underwater. The American dipper also produces oils that line its feathers, helping the feathers shed water and thus keep the bird warm.

The Grand Tour

Yosemite has so much to do and see that knowing where to start or how to get to everything can be a challenge. Fortunately, the park has bus tours that eliminate the stress of scheduling an itinerary, fighting traffic, and worrying if something important was missed. Short, area-specific tours can be taken, but tourists wanting to hit nearly all the marquee attractions can take the Grand Tour. This full-day tour makes stops at Yosemite Valley, Glacier Point, and the Mariposa Grove and gives visitors adequate time to take in scenery and snap photos of the park's most famous waterfalls, rock formations, and giant trees.

Yosemite's Other Valley

With Yosemite Valley as renowned as it is, Yosemite's other valley, Hetch Hetchy, is often overlooked. Hikers wanting to escape the crowds on the most popular trails might consider the hike to Wapama Falls

along the Hetch Hetchy Reservoir. This moderately strenuous trail covers a little more than 2.5 miles (4 km) one way, passing 2 smaller waterfalls and ending at Wapama Falls, where water plummets about 1,400 feet (427 m) over 3 drops. Although not the biggest waterfall in Yosemite, it is among the most forceful, and springtime visitors are likely to get drenched by spray as the falls hit the rocks.

Record-Setting Attractions

Less than a two-hour drive south of Yosemite are Kings Canyon National Park and Sequoia National Park. The two parks share a border and are often thought of as a single destination. Located in the Sierra Nevadas, they share many natural characteristics with Yosemite but have enough unique features to make a visit worthwhile. The canyon that gives Kings Canyon its name has a maximum depth of about 8,200 feet (2,500 m)—deeper than Arizona's Grand Canyon. Sequoia features Crystal Cave, which contains complex mineral formations, and boasts the General Sherman Tree, a 275-foot-tall (84 m) sequoia that, measured by trunk volume, is the largest known tree in the world.

High-Mountain Lake

Forested mountain roads can take Yosemite tourists north to Lake Tahoe in four to five hours. Located within the Sierra Nevadas, this glacial lake

sits more than a mile (1.6 km) above sea level, covers about 190 square miles (492 sq km), and has a maximum depth of nearly a third of a mile (500 m), making it North America's largest mountain lake and the second-deepest lake in the U.S. Tahoe's sloping shorelines are rimmed with pine and fir trees that are backdropped by impressive mountain peaks, and the lake and surrounding area are popular year round for both their scenery and recreational activities such as boating, hiking, mountain biking, and skiing.

Deterring Yosemite's Bears

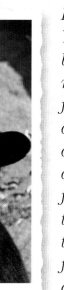

From a park that once fed bears garbage, Yosemite has become one of the most bear-cautious parks in the U.S., but visitors must do their part. The park has bear-proof food storage boxes in campgrounds as well as near parking lots. Black bears possess a sense of smell several times better than a bloodhound's, allowing them to sniff out food in vehicles, and they have the strength to break into cars. When out and about in the park, people generally do not need to fear bears, but making noise while hiking can ensure that visitors don't startle one at an uncomfortably close range.

Harder Than It Looks

Many serious rock climbers use a lot of equipment, including ropes and harnesses, while scaling rock walls. In a popular climbing activity called bouldering, climbers don't use ropes or harnesses, instead climbing closer to the ground. To an unknowing onlooker, this may seem a simple, casual activity, but bouldering requires know-how and physical conditioning. It is potentially dangerous, even to experienced climbers, and should not be imitated by novices. Every year, about

100 rock-climbing-related injuries occur within Yosemite, many of them sustained by unqualified climbers. Would-be boulderers are much better off paying for monitored climbing lessons offered within the park.

Glossary

backcountry: an area that is away from developed or populated areas

deciduous: describing plants that shed their leaves in the fall

DNA: the abbreviation for "deoxyribonucleic acid," a substance found in all organisms that carries genetic information

ecosystem: a community of animals, plants, and other living things interacting together within an environment

endemic: native and limited to a particular country or region

entrepreneur: a person who initiates new business undertakings or ideas

eroded: worn away by the action of natural forces such as water, wind, or ice

fault: a prominent break in the rock layers that make up Earth's crust; shifts or fractures may happen there, causing earthquakes or the growth of mountains

hydroelectric power: electricity produced when water movement turns turbines connected to generators

militia: an army composed of citizens rather than professional soldiers that may be called into service in times of emergency

monolith: a single, large block or piece of solid stone

nomadic: describing people who move frequently to new locations in order to obtain food, water, and shelter

plateaus: areas of high ground with a fairly level surface

prescribed burns: fires that are intentionally ignited and contained within a designated area as a means of reducing fire hazards or promoting new plant growth

reservoir: a natural or artificial lake or pond in which water is collected and stored for use

vertebrate: describing animals with a backbone or spinal column; this group includes mammals, birds, reptiles, amphibians, and fish

Selected Bibliography

Benson, Sara. *Yosemite and Sequoia/Kings Canyon National Parks*. New York: Random House, 2009.

Brower, Kenneth. *Yosemite: An American Treasure*. Washington, D.C.: National Geographic Society, 1990.

Christensen, Shane, et al. *National Parks of the American West*. New York: Wiley Publishing, 2010.

National Geographic Guide to the National Parks of the United States. Washington, D.C.: National Geographic Society, 2009.

Peterson, Eric. *Yosemite and Sequoia/Kings Canyon National Parks*. New York: Wiley Publishing, 2010.

Schullery, Paul. *America's National Parks: The Spectacular Forces That Shaped Our Treasured Lands*. New York: DK Publishing, 2001.

White, Mel. *Complete National Parks of the United States*. Washington, D.C.: National Geographic Society, 2009.

Websites

National Geographic: Yosemite National Park
http://travel.nationalgeographic.com/travel/national-parks/yosemite-national-park/
This site provides a concise visitor's guide to Yosemite, complete with maps, photos, sightseeing suggestions, and links to other popular national parks.

Yosemite National Park
http://www.nps.gov/yose/index.htm
The official National Park Service site for Yosemite is the most complete online source for information on the park and includes daily news updates.

Index